God has a plan for

Benjamin and Kaleb Robinson

_____

From: GREAT GRANDPA Earl Poysti

2008 Estes Park, Colorado

The plans of the LORD stand firm forever,
the purposes of his heart through all generations.

PSALM 33:11

God Has a Plan FOR *Little Boys*

PAINTINGS BY

Kathryn Andrews Fincher

Text by Janna Walkup

HARVEST HOUSE PUBLISHERS

EUGENE, OREGON

God Has a Plan for Little Boys
Artwork Copyright © 2008 by Kathryn Andrews Fincher
Text Copyright © 2008 by Harvest House Publishers
Published by Harvest House Publishers
Eugene, OR 97402
www.harvesthousepublishers.com

ISBN-13: 978-0-7369-2152-7
ISBN-10: 0-7369-2152-4

Design and production by Koechel Peterson & Associates, Inc.,
Minneapolis, Minnesota

Printed in Thailand

08 09 10 11 12 13 / IM / 10 9 8 7 6 5 4 3 2 1

The word of the LORD came to me, saying,
"Before I formed you in the womb I knew you,
before you were born I set you apart;
I appointed you as a prophet to the nations."
"Ah, Sovereign LORD," I said, "I do not know how to speak.
I am only a child." But the LORD said to me,
"Do not say, 'I am only a child.' You must go to everyone
I send you to and say whatever I command you.
Do not be afraid of them, for I am with you
and will rescue you," declares the LORD.

JEREMIAH 1:4–8

This book is dedicated to pastor, author, and speaker Dr. Henry Blackaby. Dr. Blackaby and I are not relatives or even close personal friends. However, Dr. Blackaby followed God's call and wrote a powerful Bible study that reached out and touched my life and the life of my high school Sunday school students. Through Dr. Blackaby's study *Experiencing God*, we all realized that we experience God's call in a daily walk and an intimate, loving relationship. God is already at work, and we are called to join Him.

This book is also dedicated to all young readers who feel a stirring in their own hearts and seek to know God's plan for their lives.

INTRODUCTION

When I was just three years old, I came upon an open can of green house paint that inspired me to try my hand at painting. But what would I paint? Aha! My four-year-old brother! My parents made sure I never created a work of art like *that* again, but the artist in me had been awakened. I drew stick figures, sketched page after page of horses, and experimented with oils to create wildlife scenes. I left trails of sketches throughout the house, but I never really thought God had a plan for me to be an artist!

Soon, I fell in love with sports. I remember the first time I stood up on water skis. I was hooked! I skied all year long—waterskiing in the summers, snow skiing in the winters. The more I skied, the better I got. Eventually, I was performing in water ski shows and even became a national water ski champion. I loved how God had given me the talent for such a fun activity.

When I married my husband, Jef, I didn't plan to have children. I wanted to keep competing in sports. But God had a different plan. I became pregnant, and little Maggie entered our life. And then little Kelley came along. *God, what is Your plan for me now?* I wondered. *I want to keep skiing, but how can I do that and be a mom at the same time?*

My husband and I started doing a study by a Bible teacher named Kay Arthur. Through this study, I realized that God had made me especially for the job of being my girls' mother. So, as I had throughout my life, I surrendered to God and allowed Him to guide me. *You know me better than I know myself, Lord,* I prayed. *I love You enough to give up my skiing, and I trust You for my future. Please show me the way.*

Soon, God made it clear that I was to return to the love of my childhood—painting. Using my own daughters and neighbor children as my models, I began to create pictures that told stories and showed people that children just like you are precious gifts from God.

When I was 9 years old, I gave my heart to Jesus. As I grew, I dreamed that God had some BIG amazing deed that He was planning for me that would *CHANGE THE WORLD!* I couldn't wait! Maybe you feel that way too. What I've discovered is that it didn't really happen for me that way. My faith and I grew up together, with one small step of faith daily. Today God has given me an important job of serving him in some BIG way, like creating this book. Yet, it was the small steps that brought me here.

As you read about the young years of these heroes that God calls to follow His plan, you will discover that what each ones does as a child matters. And what you do matters too. Why? Because each small step of faith will prepare you to become the person God created you to be.

For God has a plan...especially for you!

Kathy Fincher

God's Warrior

COME ON, LITTLE BOY," taunted the giant. "Fight me if you dare!"

The boy's grip tightened on his shepherd's stick as he fingered the five stones in his pocket, searching for one just the perfect size for his slingshot. He'd gone down to the army camp to deliver food to his brothers, who were helping the king fight yet another battle. The youngest son in his family, he usually spent his days leading his father's sheep and lambs to fresh, new grass—not fighting well-trained soldiers like this nine-foot giant.

But the boy was always up for a challenge. Sure, he spent much of his time in the fields playing his harp and singing. He loved the way music made him feel so close to God. Yet the life of a shepherd wasn't always peaceful. He'd used just his shepherd's stick and his bare hands to fight off the animals—lions, bears, and others—that tried to steal his flock. He knew that God was with him, that He was his source of strength.

He also had become very skilled with a slingshot. Days and nights out in the field gave him plenty of chances to practice. And so, with his trusty slingshot and his trust in God, he agreed to meet the giant in one-on-one combat.

The king pleaded with the boy to wear the armor he'd supplied and to use the army's best weapons. Surely the boy didn't stand a chance against this confident warrior who was fully decked out in bronzed armor and who towered above them all. At best, wearing the armor would give the boy the slightest chance of not being killed.

"I don't need it," said the boy, casting the too-big helmet and heavy shield aside. "God is with me. He's all I need." And he walked toward the giant, confidently placing a stone in the sling and drawing it back. The giant roared with laughter and held up his sword.

One shot was all it took. Suddenly the battlefield grew strangely silent as all eyes turned upon the great warrior, now lying still on the ground. The enemy army panicked. What power had this young shepherd invoked? Without even bothering to gather their belongings, the enemy turned and fled. The victory belonged to God's people. They cheered, amazed at the strength and courage of the shepherd boy and inspired to praise God for His triumph.

The strength shown by the young shepherd on that day served him well during his forty-year reign over the kingdom of Israel. Known as "a man after God's own heart," King David never wavered in his love for the Lord, and despite a life filled with adventure, he remained faithful to God just as God remained faithful to him. God had a plan for David the shepherd boy, whose bravery came from above.

And God has a plan for you as you stand strong in your faith. ⊱

+ + + + + + + + + + + + + + + +

The LORD is my strength and my shield;
my heart trusts in him, and I am helped.
My heart leaps for joy
and I will give thanks to him in song.

PSALM 28:7

+ + + + + + + + + + + + + + + +

The LORD is my *light* and my salvation—
whom shall I fear?
The LORD is the stronghold of my *life*—
of whom shall I be afraid?

PSALM 27:1

God's Leader

"OH, THANK YOU, FATHER!" the boy pulled on the brightly colored coat his father had just given him. It was a beautiful coat, to be sure—the richly dyed colors, the fine weave, the intricate pattern. But the boy's eyes were shining because he knew what receiving such a coat meant—that he was truly special in his father's eyes, that his father entrusted the family's wealth and property to him.

Usually, the father would give such a coat to the eldest son in the family. To be the eleventh son and to receive such a gift was unheard of.

His brothers were already jealous of the favor their father had shown to their next-to-youngest brother when a dream that the boy had further enraged them.

"In my dream," he told his brothers, "you all bowed down to me."

"We must do something," said one of the brothers after they had sent their brother wearing the colorful coat out to another part of the valley. "He thinks he's so much better than the rest of us. Let's get rid of him."

"Yes," agreed another brother. "We can put him in that pit over there."

Blessed are those who hunger
and thirst for **righteousness**,
for they **will** be filled.

MATTHEW 5:6

+ + + + + + + + + + + + + + + +

*B*ut seek first his kingdom
and his righteousness,
and all these things will be given
to you as well.

MATTHEW 6:33

+ + + + + + + + + + + + + + + +

After he had been in the pit awhile, the
brothers saw some merchants headed for Egypt.
Suddenly one of the brothers had an idea.

"We can sell you a good slave at a cheap
price," he told the merchants, who were
indeed in need of someone to help them on
their journey. The merchants gladly bought
the boy, but not before his brothers had first

stolen away his coat. On the way home, they dipped the coat in some goat's blood.

Trying to appear sad, the brothers approached their father. "We found this coat out in the fields. It's our brother's, isn't it?"

The father nodded sadly, believing that his favorite son had been killed by a wild animal. *He was such a good boy,* the father thought. *So smart, and with such a heart for God. I always thought that something special was in store for him. Now what? Who can take his place?*

Meanwhile, the boy was having similar thoughts. He knew that God had told him he would someday be put in a high position, but how could this be? He was on his way to another country—as a slave! Yet he didn't complain or try to escape from his captors.

He worked hard as a slave and became well-known for telling people what their dreams meant. The king, pleased with his honesty and intelligence, put him in charge of all the food in Egypt. At first the job was easy, for the harvests were good and the people had plenty. But then came a period where the crops did not grow, and soon people even

from faraway lands came to the king's storehouse to buy grain.

When the boy's brothers came to Egypt, the boy—now an important man who enjoyed considerable power in the house of the king—recognized them immediately. Having forgiven them long ago, he smiled to himself as he saw God's hand at work in all that had unfolded in their lives.

The brothers were afraid when they realized who this man actually was. What would he to do to them? But they need not have worried. Their brother saw how sorry they were for what they did, and he had forgiven them long ago.

Even though it didn't seem like it when Joseph was sold by his brothers and taken to Egypt as a slave, God had a plan for him. Never questioning God and always doing what was right, Joseph held fast to God's promises and was grateful that he was in a position to help feed his family.

As Joseph kept his eyes fixed on a heavenly kingdom, so also can you continue to do what is right in the eyes of God, knowing that He has something special in store for you. ✄

*Firm, **faithful**, and devoted, full of energy and **zeal**, and **truth**, he labors for his race...*

CHARLOTTE BRONTE

God's Olympian

OU CAN'T CATCH ME!" The boy ran, blond hair flying in the breeze. How he loved a game of chase! Any game that involved running—tag, football, even following a butterfly. God had made him fast, he knew. But his gift of speed was just one thing among many. He was most thankful that God was so good and that He had given him parents who cared so much about not only their own children but all of God's children.

Born to a mother and father who were Scottish missionaries stationed in China, the boy spent his first five years running with his Chinese playmates. When he turned six, he and his eight-year-old brother were sent to England to attend a boarding school for the sons of missionaries.

The boy's athletic ability and agreeable nature quickly won him many friends at his new school. He soon learned the games of rugby and cricket, and before long he became captain of each squad on which he played and won many Best Athlete awards. Yet his success never changed his kind personality. "He's entirely without vanity," said his headmaster approvingly.

Soon he became known as the best runner in the country, earning the nickname of the Flying Scotsman. The 1924 Olympic Games were just around the corner, and no athlete from Scotland had ever won an Olympic gold medal before. But maybe, just maybe, this year would be different. For the boy—now a college student—was incredibly fast, especially in the 100 meters. Running with his head thrust into the sky, he insisted that God was the one who showed him the finish line. "The Lord guides me," he said.

As the Olympics drew closer, he trained harder and harder while at the same time working diligently at his studies, competing in races, and speaking at many meetings. He was shy and didn't enjoy talking to large groups, but he was becoming famous for his athletic accomplishments. People begged him to speak, and he agreed. He never spoke about his triumphs; instead, he talked about God and how he experienced his heavenly Father's love and support each and every day.

+ + + + + + + + + + + + + + + +

He gives strength to the weary
and increases the power of the weak.
Even youths grow tired and weary,
and young men stumble and fall;
but those who hope in the LORD
will renew their strength.
They will soar on wings like eagles;
they will run and not grow weary.

ISAIAH 40:29–31

+ + + + + + + + + + + + + + + +

When the schedule for the track and field events was published several months before the start of the Olympics, he discovered that his specialty—the 100 meters—would be run on a Sunday. He'd trained his whole life for this moment, but he knew immediately that the gold medal was not his to win. Sunday was a day to worship God, not a day to compete for earthly glory. He withdrew his name from the event.

Everyone assumed that Scotland's first hope for gold was finished. But the gifted runner with a heart for God shifted his focus to another race—the 400 meters, which was *not* being run on a Sunday. He wasn't favored to win, but he made his way through the qualifying heats of the race, not clocking the fastest times but running fast enough to advance to the next round. At that time, the record in the event was 48.2 seconds.

When he broke the tape at the finish line of the Olympic final, he was five meters ahead of the nearest runner. He had covered the 400-meter course in 47.6 seconds and brought home the gold to the cheers of the Scottish people and the entire world.

God had a plan for Eric Liddell, the missionaries' son whom God rewarded for his faithfulness. While his competitors were running the 100 meters in the 1924 Paris Olympics, he was speaking in a church. The man made famous in the film *Chariots of Fire* lived as he ran—always focused, always faithful.

So keep running the race God has placed you in, eyes straight ahead on the wonderful things He has planned for you. ✄

Therefore, since we are surrounded by such a great cloud of witnesses, let us throw off everything that hinders and the sin that so easily entangles, and let us run with perseverance the race marked out for us.

HEBREWS 12:1

God's Messenger

THE TWELVE-YEAR-OLD boy took a deep breath. "Father, Mother, I've decided that I want to be a pastor when I grow up," he announced. He knew this wasn't what his parents imagined he would do with his life. Very smart and determined, the boy had been expected to follow in his father's footsteps as a doctor and university professor.

His parents weren't thrilled by the boy's choice. They had given him and his eight siblings a privileged life in their Berlin home. Homeschooled by their mother and surrounded by the best books and music in their luxuri-ous home, the children were expected to make something of their lives. A simple pastor wasn't what they had envisioned this brilliant boy becom-ing, but they respected his choice and did not stand in his way.

Beginning his study of theology at age fourteen, he was well on his way to becoming a Lutheran pastor. Preaching and teaching, along with writing and study, became a way of life for him. And yet God was prepar-ing him for much more than a career.

When the Nazis came to power in Germany, this pastor with a heart tuned to Christ knew that something

On thee alone my *hope* relies;
Beneath thy cross I fall,
My **Lord**, my life, my sacrifice,
My Savior, and my all.

ANNE STEELE

was very wrong. Sadly, many of his friends and fellow pastors did not see the evil he saw in this powerful man Hitler. And as he continued to share the gospel, he realized more and more how starkly Hitler's treatment of the Jews contrasted with Christ's love and mercy for all people. In fact, he had been suspicious of the German leader from the first week he came to power.

And so he began to speak out against Hitler, organizing his own church—the Confessing Church—when the Nazis took control of the official German state church. "My calling is quite clear to me," he said. "What God will make of it I do not know . . . I must follow the path."

The Nazis soon became suspicious of this bold preacher who dared to speak out against their regime. First they banned him from preaching. Next they forbid him to teach. Finally they told him he could not do any kind of public speaking. When they still couldn't silence him, they arrested him and put him in prison.

Unwilling to renounce his faith, he suffered so evil would be defeated. Before the Nazis took his life, he spoke words that showed who was the true Leader of his heart: "This is the end. For me, the beginning of life."

God had a plan for Dietrich Bonhoeffer. The boy determined to become a pastor eventually preached to the whole world a message about truly living out your beliefs. In life and in death, he answered the call of God.

Like Dietrich Bonhoeffer, let all that you do in your life point to God, who has made you for a purpose. ✂

+ + + + + + + + + + + + + + + + +

There are in every generation
those who shrink from the ultimate sacrifice,
but there are in every generation those
who make it with joy and laughter
and these are the salt of the generations.

PATRICK HENRY PEASE

+ + + + + + + + + + + + + + + + +

No, no, we are not *satisfied*, and we will not be satisfied until *justice* rolls down like waters and righteousness like a *mighty* stream.

MARTIN LUTHER KING JR.

God's Dream Keeper

THE BOY SAT in the chair in the front of the shoe store, swinging his legs back and forth and eagerly anticipating how a shiny new pair of shoes would look on his feet. He and his father had come downtown together, just the two of them. When the clerk approached, the boy got ready to tell him what size he needed. But the clerk wasn't interested in helping the boy find a pair of shoes. "You have to get your shoes there," he told the boy and his father rudely, gesturing to the back of the store.

The boy's father stood up. "We will either buy our shoes right here, or we will not buy them in this store at all," he informed the clerk.

When the clerk shrugged and turned away, the father took his son's hand, and together they walked out of the store, heads held high.

The scene in the shoe store made no sense to the boy. His father had the money. He needed shoes. They were good customers, so why were they standing out here on the street with the money still in his father's wallet and the old shoes still on the boy's feet?

The scene reminded him of what had happened with his friends. He'd grown accustomed to playing with the two little boys whose parents ran the store across the street from the big white and gray house in which he lived. One day, soon after the storekeeper's sons had started attending a school in a different neighborhood, they'd refused to play with him. When he asked the parents why their boys couldn't play, they had replied, "Because you're colored."

The boy knew that his skin was darker than that of his friends, but it hadn't made any difference until now. And as he thought about it, he noticed other things that didn't seem right—like how black people and white people had separate drinking fountains. And how a black person was expected to sit in the back of the bus or give up his or her seat for a white person. Weren't all people—black and white—created in God's image and loved by Him? Why did they need to be separated to get a drink of water, to ride a bus, or to play or buy shoes?

His father and his grandfather, men of God who were deeply troubled by the things that weren't right in the world, had both chosen to become Baptist ministers. They had devoted their lives to helping all of God's people, to working for change and what was right. This, the boy decided, was something worth committing his life to.

Bright and motivated, he entered college at the age of fifteen and went on to receive advanced degrees. He met his wife at Boston University, and when they married they returned to the South to minister to a Baptist church in Montgomery, Alabama.

God put him in the right place at the right time. When he and his wife arrived in

Blessed are the peacemakers,
for they will be called sons of God.

MATTHEW 5:9

Alabama, they saw two separate worlds—clearly, a better world for whites than for blacks. And so he began to speak up for change, for equality, for justice. He organized protests. He gave inspired speeches. He brought people together to work for what was fair. And he never gave up his dream.

God had a plan for Martin Luther King Jr., leader of the American civil rights movement and winner of the Nobel Peace Prize, a true peacemaker who inspired Americans everywhere to fight for an end to racial injustice.

As Martin Luther King Jr. learned from his own father to notice and do something about the things that aren't right in the world, you too can stand up for what is just, knowing that God has created you to do good things.

++++++++++++++++++

*N*othing in the world
can take the place of Persistence.
Talent will not; nothing is more common
than unsuccessful men with talent.
Genius will not; unrewarded genius
is almost a proverb. Education will not;
the world is full of educated derelicts.
Persistence and Determination alone
are omnipotent. The slogan "Press On"
has solved and will always solve
the problems of the human race.

CALVIN COOLIDGE

++++++++++++++++++

Courage, brother! do not stumble,
Though thy path be dark as night;
There's a star to guide the **humble,**
Trust in **God** and do the Right.

NORMAN MACLEOD

The Lord is good, a refuge in times of trouble. He cares for those who trust in him.

NAHUM 1:7

God's Smuggler

*M*OM, BROTHER snuck out of church *again!*"

The boy's mother groaned, wondering what was to become of her obviously bright yet wayward son. He seemed so against the things of God, becoming upset when she sang a hymn or even when someone said grace at the table. But she had other worries. Her husband, a poor blacksmith, worked hard to support her and their six children. And now there was a war on.

She had to suppress a giggle, though, when she thought of the boy's pranks. When he was younger, he was always playing one trick or another on his brothers. Now, he'd made the German soldiers the targets of his mischief. She remembered the time a German general had become angry when his car wouldn't work. He'd seemed so confused when the mechanics had suggested there was sugar in the gasoline. Just that morning she'd noticed that the sugar bowl had seemed suddenly empty, but she hadn't said anything at all.

The war ended, but the boy's restlessness didn't. He joined the army and went overseas to fight, not caring about his life and not having anything in particular for which to live. He was wounded in the ankle, but he survived. Forced to spend a lengthy period of time recovering in a hospital, he began to read the Bible. He read God's Word cover to cover—and then he read it again. Suddenly, the boy who had not been able to tolerate a church service or even a mealtime prayer could not get enough of the Scriptures.

He committed his life to Christ, vowing to do whatever God wished for him to do. Always ready for adventure and still having a nose for mischief, he was drawn to the lands where Christians were being persecuted. In these places, people weren't supposed to even own a Bible. And so he determined to bring God's Word to them.

Traveling in a battered Volkswagen Beetle, he packed tracts and Bibles into his suitcases and began smuggling them into the countries that were most antagonistic toward God's Word. He determined to open up these countries for Christ as his own heart had been opened.

Amazing things began to happen. His broken-down car traveled great distances on dusty roads, astonishing mechanics who declared that such a vehicle shouldn't have lasted a mile. He trusted fully in God, often placing Bibles on the dashboard in full view of the guards. "Lord, please make seeing eyes blind," became his prayer. And God was always faithful to answer it.

God had a plan for Brother Andrew, "God's smuggler," who began his mission with one suitcase full of God's Word and eventually, through the Open Door Mission, brought the message of salvation to more than sixty countries.

As you allow God to work in your life, He will guide your footsteps. He has a plan for you. ✄

+ + + + + + + + + + + + + + + + +

Trust in the LORD with all your heart
and lean not on your own understanding;
in all your ways acknowledge him,
and he will make your paths straight.

PROVERBS 3:5–6

+ + + + + + + + + + + + + + + + +

God's Companion

THE BOY WAS RAISED in a Christian home with loving parents who made God a priority in their lives. His aunt and uncle served as missionaries in China, and he delighted in hearing stories of how the Chinese people came to know Jesus. Faith was always a part of his family, and he wondered from a young age what God wanted him to do with his own life.

When he was nine years old, though, he had an encounter with God that would shape the rest of his life. Used to praying for direction in his life, he once again asked God, "Lord, what is it that you want me to be? What do you want me to do?"

The answer was not what he'd expected. "I don't want you to do anything," God replied. "I want you to experience Me. I want you to be in a relationship with Me, to get to know Me. I want you to know that you are always surrounded by My love."

From this point on, the boy realized that God's plan had already been set in motion and that he simply needed to become a part of that plan. He would do this by drawing nearer to the Lord, spending time with Him every day and basking in His loving presence.

Humility opens the door to *faith*; *pride closes it.*

KATHY FINCHER

Although he grew up in a loving Christian home, walking with God wasn't always easy. As a teenager, he often found himself alone in his faith, the only one willing to live life for a heavenly purpose. Blessed with height and athletic ability, the boy was drawn to the game of basketball. He eventually joined an elite team, which played against squads including the Harlem Globetrotters. As the only Christian on his team, the boy was asked by the coach to lead the team in prayer. Instead of feeling singled out and different from the other players, he was instead always grateful that God could speak through him in this way.

The boy who had once asked God what he needed to do learned that the most important thing in life was to know God—to experience Him, to enjoy Him, to walk and talk with Him, to pray with Him. He learned to trust God in each and every moment of his life, never looking for things ahead of time, always trusting that God was showing him the way as he walked in faith.

God had a plan for Henry Blackaby, the boy who realized that it was not about him— it was about God. He discovered that it wasn't about what he could do *for* God but rather about what he could do *with* and *through* Him. His Bible study *Experiencing God*, along with other well-known studies, has inspired countless believers all over the world—including the Masi warriors in Africa—to live their lives humbly and joyfully walking in the Lord's presence.

Like Henry Blackaby, you can live your life knowing that God has a plan for this world— and that you're an important part of it. ✄

++++++++++++++++++

He guides the humble
in what is right
and teaches them his way.

PSALM 25:9

++++++++++++++++++